Single-seat twin-float monoplane.
Power-one Rolls-Royce 'R' twelve cylinder.
Vee-type piston engine (2550 h.p.).
Wing span — 9.14 m. (30 ft. 0 in.).
Length — 8.79 m. (28 ft. 10 in.).
Height — 3.73 m. (12 ft. 3 in.).

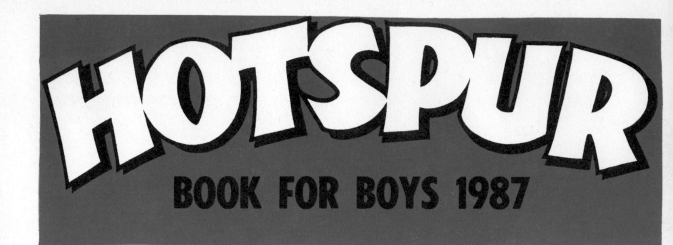

HOTSPUR
BOOK FOR BOYS 1987

CONTENTS

Black Jack's Private Army 5
Louis The Loser 15
One-Minute Murphy 17
Custer At The Charge 26
Bertie's Bear 33
Cast, Hook and Strike 42
Game Fish 49
Kestrel 50
Ossie The Outlaw 61
Hotch Potch 64

Victoria Cross Crossing 65
How Was I To Know He Was A General? 74
Hurricane Hutch 81
Mountie Muldoon 91
The Beckoning Peak 94
It's A Funny Old World 96
King Cobra 97
The Slowest Gun In The West 105
The Gloster Gladiator 113
X-Bow 117

Printed and Published in Great Britain by D. C. THOMSON & CO., LTD.,
185 Fleet Street, London EC4A 2HS.
© D. C. THOMSON & CO., LTD., 1986.
ISBN 0 85116 367 X

The captives were escorted up the bluff . . .

You go in hole we dig for you.

It wasn't my fault it was a duff mine, Kibaw. I paid your people well considering I didn't scratch out more than a handful of poor grade rubies.

What now, Uncle Jack? We're solidly locked in!

We'll start with you not sitting on that box of old dynamite, Tommy. It could be dodgy!

Thought so—it's sweating. These drops are pure nitro-glycerine explosive.

Later, other visitors came to the Payah . . .

Noble one, we greet you in friendship.

That is good—and just as well for you!

Crumbs! It's dodgy all right!

POP SNAP CRACKLE

It is well that you are friendly!

AEEI!

9

So you changed your mind about that deal, old friend.

It is so, Jacko. I find that we Payah are not good at obedience. We will help you fight the Japoni!

Jack instructed Kibaw and his warriors in firing the captured Jap weapons. Jack was in a hurry to hit back at the Japs — and soon he had chosen his first ambush site.

The bend of the river makes a perfect ambush, chaps. You soon got the hang of this Jap gun, Sher Khan.

Was I not in the Tochi Scouts, huzoor?

Cease firing! That burst proved we can reach everything in sight from here.

Dusk settled . . .

Engine noise on the river! Douse those fires!

Huzoor, the noise comes from the upper river. It cannot be the Japs.

Ahoy! Uncle Jack!

Young Tommy! I told the brat to stay up at the Payah village.

I brought that paraffin oil from the old mission. We could pour it on the river and set it on fire when the Japs come.

Our small sahib has some good notions, huzoor.

Never heard anything so dashed unsporting in me life. Tommy, you can take that stuff back upriver this minute. Those Japs are going to be slaughtered decently with lead and steel.

Let me stay, Uncle. I feel safer with you.

Very well, but try not to get in the way, young 'un.

See many Japoni—big boats. Make camp on creek of barking deer!

That means they'll be here about mid-morning. We'll be ready for 'em.

Next morning . . .

Mirror-flash from scouts. Japoni in sight.

Check on your chaps, Kibaw. I want no firing till the machine-gun opens up!

A mortar bomb! Where the deuce did that come from?

11

I need a way of igniting this paraffin oil.

Huzoor, there is an oil lamp in the cabin.

They're firing wild! We got 'em rattled, Sher Khan!

Huzoor, even the Tochi Scouts were never like this!

Prepare to ram! Lash your helm.

Abandon ship!

The craft collided . . .

The paraffin drums explode!

Remarkable! Wonder if that Admiral Lord Nelson-wallah used the same stuff on the Frogs!

The enemy steam-launch foundered . . .

Behold, huzoor! The barges are helpless without their tow. The current sweeps them. The Japs will never catch our villagers!

Jack and Sher Khan caught up with the canoe flotilla . . .

See, Payah arrows have won the guns of the Japoni behind us!

Well done, Kibaw! They'll come in handy for my little army.

Jacko, you are great warrior. Payah proud to be in your army and chase the Japoni from our country!

Jolly good show, Kibaw. Must be a born leader of men, doncher know—

—fire or sword, it all comes the same in the end. But it takes a great commander to know which one to choose!

I thought you said fire was unsporting, Uncle Jack.

Tommy, shut up. There are times when, like the great Admiral Lord Nelson, one has to turn a blind eye to the finer things when one is at war!

The End

LOUIS THE LOSER

I'm bored! This whole town is a dump!

Louis was down in the dumps...

Louis! If you've nothing better to do, you can help your Gran clear out her attic!

Yes, Mum! But that's even worse than being bored!

GROOUGH! COUGH! The dust's going for me already! What a rotten start to the day... but at least it can only get better.

You can keep anything you fancy, Louis! Throw everything else away!

This vase doesn't look too bad. I'll take it to Rummy's Hill-Top Antiques—with the rest of the stuff from here.

Later...

Nothing there worth buying except this jug. It's a good one. How much do you want for it?

I... er... dunno... er...

He's selling others like it... I'll ask for a price in between.

How about five pounds!

Done!

I knew I'd come out on top... Ha, ha, ha! I'm not a loser—I'm a born winner!

15

ONE-MINUTE MURPHY

ANDY MURPHY had just joined First Division, Clinton United, where his brother, Joe, was manager. But Mr Hagley, the club chairman, did not like Andy's unorthodox style . . .

Okay, kids, I'll get your ball back for you!

Hey, that's Andy Murphy, the United's new striker!

Come and join us, Andy! Show us how you nip through defences on your own!

Here I come, then!

What do you know? I've taken the ball off Andy Murphy!

Oops!

It's not supposed to be that easy! You're reckoned to be a star First Division striker!

Where's he gone?

There's some argument about that! But I had my mind on other things. Let that be a lesson to you! When you've got the ball, concentrate on it! Let's try again!

Wow! Clean through the lot! That's more like it! Great stuff, Andy!

Andy, I've been looking all over for you! You're wanted back at the ground!

I've told you, if you keep on arguing with Hagley about me, you'll end up getting the sack, Joe. So I'd better quit!

Not yet you don't! There's a meeting of our board of directors due soon, and I want you to be there!

Oh, all right! Thanks for the game, lads!

Later... I've told you, Murphy, your brother doesn't give the all-out effort I want. For most of the game, he just idles about! We don't pay a player for one minute's work!

In that one minute he scores! And, if you drop him, you pay him for doing nothing at all, Mr Hagley! Andy's got a six-month contract!

We'll take a vote on it. Who's in favour of keeping Murphy on our playing strength?

Three of the directors! And you and the other two against! You're evenly divided, Mr Hagley.

Half of you want Andy in the team against Ridley City on Saturday, and the other half don't. I suggest a compromise, Mr Hagley. We'll name Andy as sub.

Very well. But I want Des Craddock as striker. Now there's a player who really grafts for the full ninety minutes!

The day of the Ridley match...

Hagley's joining us to keep an eye on you, Joe. If you pull Craddock off and put me on, he'll accuse you of getting your own way by back-door methods!

Craddock will be all out to impress. And, if I know Craddock, that means Hagley will be agreeing to a substitution before the end of the match!

The match started...

Mine! I'm going to show them!

Foul!

Craddock's trying to batter his way through with brute force and ignorance. He'd better watch that ref!

The lad's just a bit over-eager. He'll settle down!

You don't beat me that easy!

Ow! Foul, ref!

Later . . .

In the middle, Des!

Right!

That was my ball you pair of ninnies!

The defence is in a right tangle! Quick Des! Hit it! It's your birthday!

What a miss! How could you have missed that one Des?

Des stabbed at it. That's the worst of these eager beavers! Andy would have put that one away nice and easy!

Des Craddock chased everything and ran frantically all over the park but to no avail. Then, with ten minutes to go . . .

My ball—aaagh!

Craddock's got the yellow card! If we don't substitute him soon, he'll be sent off and we'll be down to ten men!

Er—yes. He is trying rather too hard. All right, Murphy, send your brother on!

The goalie's taking the free kick. This is mine if I move fast.

Crikey, where did he come from?

Murphy's away!

Goal!

One-Minute Murphy again! Straight on, and he scores, before anybody else can touch the ball!

After scoring his goal, Andy seemed to disappear from the game . . .

Get into the game, Murphy! Don't hang about!

Get on with it, Murphy. I'm supposed to be a spectator, not you!

The goalie puts most of his long kicks there—

—and he turns his back on the game after a long clearance. A bad habit that. It could cost him!

22

Look at that brother of yours loitering about, the great idle lump!

But Andy was not as idle as he looked and, a few minutes later, he exploded into action . . .

Goalies should really vary their kicks!

Hey, what—

Don't worry! It's only me! You shouldn't take things for granted, mate!

Watch out, Bert!

Hey, where did that come from?

Goalies can't afford to get careless!

How about that, then, Mr Hagley?

Aw, he just got lucky. It was a chance in a million that wild swipe at the ball went in.

23

Keep your crosses low, Ernie. These high balls are just a gift to old Jack the Beanstalk.

Okay, Skipper! I'll remember!

Jack Barstock's having an easy afternoon. He's mopping up all the high balls. People are hardly bothering to challenge. I wonder . . .

Next time you break down the right, Ernie, put over a high, hanging cross!

But I can't, Andy! You heard what the Skipper just said!

Never mind that! Just do it!

And, a few minutes later . . .

This is money for old rope!

Here goes!

Hey, what—

Made it! Jack the Beanstalk had it so easy he got over-confident!

The End

25

CUSTER at the CHARGE

"SO there I was, peace-loving old me, dodging Ye Glue Factorye by serving as war-horse of the dauntless Sir Waldo Twitch in that rumble with those Roundheads. Anyway, we were between battle fixtures when the Hon. Coney Clapper led out Sir Waldo and a few of the boys on a forage for vital supplies . . . oysters for Prince Rudolph . . ."

. . . when we sighted these Ironsides . . .

Gentlemen, if you please—HALT! We have something to discuss . . .

Such heavy odds offer us a splendid chance of winning a little glory, Coney, old friend.

Humph—er, quite, Sir Waldo. Yet this ground be ill-suited to skirmishing.

27

Waldo was waking up when I got him back to camp . . .

My brave fellow, your friends have told how valorously you drew off an army of Round-heads to save them and my oysters.

Huh—er, I did, Your Highness.

Excellent, My Lord Ragwort. In the morrow's battle, the standard of your troop shall be borne by Sir Waldo.

Highness, Twitch could be promoted to cornet. I'm always losing them.

The rightful place for such a valiant soldier is forward where the action be hottest.

I didn't like what I was hearing.

Next morning, I reported sick . . .

The poor fellow is most unwell, Coney. I could barely coax a half sack of oats down him.

Not to worry, Twitch, I have the surest physic for curing a drooping old nag!

Just blow into his gizzard this ball of me special recipe of foxglove and gunpowder mixed with a fair splash of castor oil. Never fails!

If that don't work, then the old nag be fit only for ye glue factorye.

Huh! Don't like the sound of that!

Ye glue factorye!

That left flank looked unhealthy to me...

I decided to stay healthy...

Don't Twitch appear to be veering off somewhat far leftish, Coney?

Sirrah, our duty be not to ask questions, but to faithfully follow yonder banner even unto death.

So they followed...

Sir Waldo wasn't paying much attention...

Yurgh... oh, me innards ... arghhh...

Urgh—glub!

I must have got my bearings mixed because suddenly we came on these wagons...

Sir, a Royalist banner!

Blood-and-bone! Those sneaky fops have outflanked us.

The powder train be better destroyed than taken.

Oddsfish, the Roundhead supply lines! We've outflanked the rascals!

Thanks to the brilliant tactics of our new cornet. But where is my dear friend?

Senseless and a trifle scorched—yet he lives. Trust him to be where the action is hottest!

Losing their gunpowder gave them Roundheads no choice except to call off the fixture . . .

Be limbering up the cannon. We advance to rearward!

Sir Waldo never could figure out how he'd done it . . .

I remember only being somewhat unwell, noble steed. It must be that at such times a fighting soldier's instincts take command of him.

Huh!

THE EN

BERTIE'S BEAR

AUGUST 1945 and the Second World War had just ended. The Japanese had surrendered and were being cleared from Burma. With the 4th Fusiliers were country boy, Private Bert Toomly, and Bozzler — the wild bear which had adopted him and become the regimental mascot . . .

Come back, Bozz, you silly ol' bear!

What the devil's that noise?

I think it's something to do with that bear, sir!

What's all this commotion, Toomly?

It's all right, sir! It's only Bozz. He raided a swill bin an' got stuck an' panicked like!

I — Ooooof!

Well done, sir! You've stopped him!

So, a few nights later, the scent of honey filled the air . . .

A few minutes later . . .

Bozzler! Where are you, Bozzler? Have you seen Bozzler, Joe?

No! Nothing came my way!

Look! He went that way! Come on, you lads. We got to get Bozzler! Besides, he's got the map!

Bozzler followed the scent of honey . . .

Now!

GRAAAAOOOH!

Bandits — Dacoits! If they've hurt Bozz . . .

We've lost the map! They've cut off his collar!

They've got a boat! They're getting away!

We can't stop 'em!

You dopey bear! You've landed us in trouble.

Bozz, come back. Don't run away! I didn't mean it!

You've upset him! He's done a bunk!

As dawn broke . . .

Careful! Take it easy! Bozzler's slowing up! Don't rush him!

For us, the war is not over! We fight on to the death! Banzai! We join others downriver.

Ouuuurr!

KRAAAK!

39

CAST, HOOK and STRIKE

Look, Grandpa! An English-style Fish and Chipper Bar. There is a queue, outside.

Just the job, Joe! Nip out and get me some fish and chips! Seems ages since we had a good fish supper!

FRANK'S OLD-FASHIONED ENGLISH FISH AND CHIPS BAR

FRYING TODAY

JOE DODDS had emigrated to Australia with his grandfather, Ernie Dodds. In partnerhip with an Australian named Merve, they ran a busy little haulage business. On their way back from a job one day . . .

FISH & CHIPS PASTIES . . . STEAK & K. PIES . . . .

Looks like the real thing. I'm looking forward to it!

A few minutes later . . .

Fish and chips and vinegar! That smell takes me back! There's a lay-by just down the road. We'll stop and eat them there!

I'm starving! If there's one thing I miss about good old England, it's me fish and chips!

Aye, you always were one for going to the chipper!

What's the matter, Grandpa?

It's that fish! I wouldn't give that rubbish to the cat!

42

43

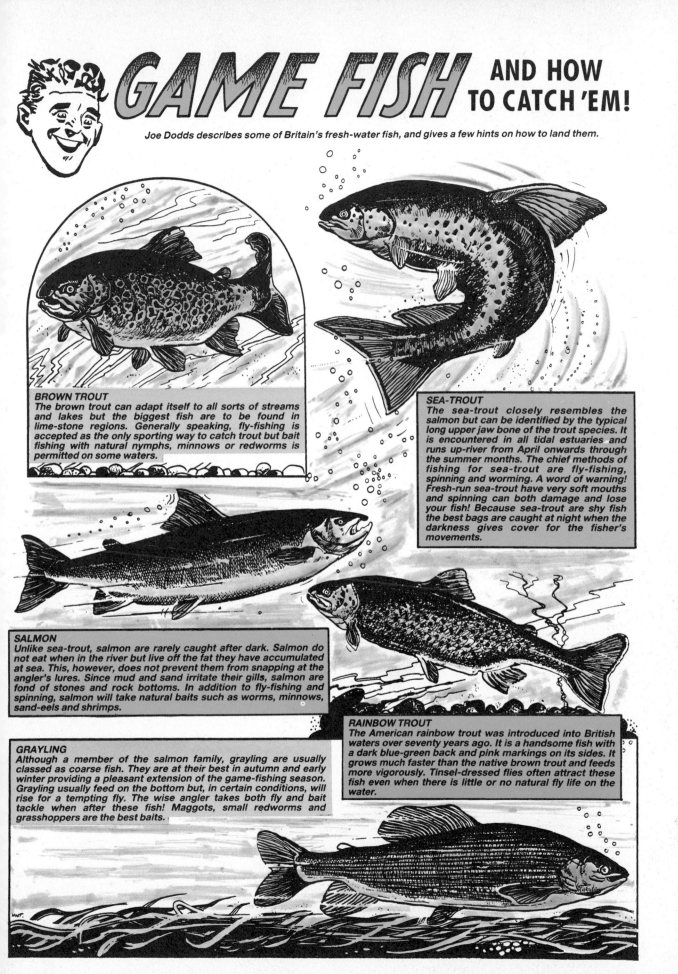

GAME FISH AND HOW TO CATCH 'EM!

Joe Dodds describes some of Britain's fresh-water fish, and gives a few hints on how to land them.

BROWN TROUT
The brown trout can adapt itself to all sorts of streams and lakes but the biggest fish are to be found in lime-stone regions. Generally speaking, fly-fishing is accepted as the only sporting way to catch trout but bait fishing with natural nymphs, minnows or redworms is permitted on some waters.

SEA-TROUT
The sea-trout closely resembles the salmon but can be identified by the typical long upper jaw bone of the trout species. It is encountered in all tidal estuaries and runs up-river from April onwards through the summer months. The chief methods of fishing for sea-trout are fly-fishing, spinning and worming. A word of warning! Fresh-run sea-trout have very soft mouths and spinning can both damage and lose your fish! Because sea-trout are shy fish the best bags are caught at night when the darkness gives cover for the fisher's movements.

SALMON
Unlike sea-trout, salmon are rarely caught after dark. Salmon do not eat when in the river but live off the fat they have accumulated at sea. This, however, does not prevent them from snapping at the angler's lures. Since mud and sand irritate their gills, salmon are fond of stones and rock bottoms. In addition to fly-fishing and spinning, salmon will take natural baits such as worms, minnows, sand-eels and shrimps.

GRAYLING
Although a member of the salmon family, grayling are usually classed as coarse fish. They are at their best in autumn and early winter providing a pleasant extension of the game-fishing season. Grayling usually feed on the bottom but, in certain conditions, will rise for a tempting fly. The wise angler takes both fly and bait tackle when after these fish! Maggots, small redworms and grasshoppers are the best baits.

RAINBOW TROUT
The American rainbow trout was introduced into British waters over seventy years ago. It is a handsome fish with a dark blue-green back and pink markings on its sides. It grows much faster than the native brown trout and feeds more vigorously. Tinsel-dressed flies often attract these fish even when there is little or no natural fly life on the water.

KESTREL

No! Jim! Jim Gable's on that plane!

KESTREL, a tough internation cop, was arriving at Lond airport to meet an old friend. the plane taxied towards the arriv terminal—

Within seconds—

Let me GO! An old friend is on that plane!

Don't be a fool. You can't go near that wreck! Hold him —he's out of his mind!

Bitter and enraged, Kestrel drove away from the airport.

What the—?

The idiot! He thinks he's on a race track.

Foolishly, Mr Parker tried to resist, and—

Ooof!

Pity you don't handle yourself as well as you do a souped-up car, pal!

Now, Mr Parker. I want to know what you were doing at the scene of the aircraft explosion AND the bombed restaurant—and I want the truth so don't give me any guff about coincidences!

Okay! Okay! Just let me breathe . . .

It's simple! I'm a reporter. Some top people were coming in on that plane—and some top people were at that restaurant. I happened to be on the spot both times because of my job.

Right! I always carry plenty of camera equipment around so I had some terrific pictures too!

Fair enough, Parker. It fits.

Tough on the people involved, but you got two hot scoops, so you put your foot down to get the stories back . . .

Kestrel put Parker out of his mind until the following day. Then, at one of the top racetracks—

Those Silver Bullet boys certainly mean business. And, once again, a lot of top people were involved. This is beginning to take on a pattern . . . I think I'll pay another call on Mr Parker!

I think you can help, Parker. You're a society reporter. You'll have lists of the top people who were on the plane, in the restaurant, and at that race-meeting. Can I see 'em?

Sure! If you're on to something I'd like to know, Kestrel—it could mean another big scoop for me.

Soon—

Hmmmm! Something very interesting about these lists. It's just a hunch, but one I could follow-up.

What is it, Kestrel? If you're on to something then let me in on it.

Not yet, pal. It's too vague. But you'll be the first to know.

I'll settle for that!

Later, as Kestrel pulled into his garage—

HEY! Who the blazes—?

Great! Now finish him! He knows too much!

Uggh!

54

55

Then—

Hey! That looks like a man with a grenade-launcher! I could be wrong but I can't afford to ignore it. I'm going up there—and fast!

I don't want to start a panic if I'm wrong—but I'd better move. But how do I get to that spot-grid?

Cat-walks and grids everywhere! Which one leads out onto that spot?

The delay was fatal! In the auditorium—

High above—

Oh, NO! I'm too late!

Then—

57

Well, at least I know now that my hunch was right. Every one of those gatherings that were hit had a member of a Middle-Eastern royal family present. The mass-killings were a blind to cover the REAL target!

Later—

Argh! Just—just saved myself—but there's no way I can catch him now . . .

Kestrel headed for Parker's home. But, as he arrived—

There's Parker now. I'll call to him—

Early the next morning—

First a word with Ken Parker. He can tell me the next function that will be attended by the fifth member of that royal family. Then I can tell the Boss and we can be ready and waiting for the attack . . .

But Kestrel spotted something that made him change his mind.

Seconds later, Kestrel was in pursuit.

Of course! What an idiot I've been! I'd better get back to my own car—and quick!

No wonder Parker was so interested in my hunch. It must have been him who tipped-off the heavies that I was on to something . . .

59

OSSIE the OUTLAW

LOOK OUT!

ALL the members of the Pringle family were outlaws and Maw Pringle was proud of them—all except young Ossie, who was no good as a badman. One day in Sludge Springs.

YOU NEED GLASSES, YOUNG FELLER. YOU SHOULD WATCH WHERE YER GOIN'.

I WAS BOWLIN' MY HOOP. I CAIN'T DO TWO THINGS AT ONCE!

HEY! HE'S DROPPED SOMETHIN'-

A PLAN! TO A GOLD MINE! BETTER GIT HOME TO MAW WITH THIS!

BANG! CRASH!

MAW! MAW! ARE YOU ALL RIGHT?

ARE YOU TRYIN' TO BE FUNNY, BOY?

GEE, I'M SORRY, MAW. HEY! LOOK AT THIS, MAW. IT'S ANOTHER TUNNEL!

MAYBE IT'S THE MAIN SHAFT!

SHEESH! SURE IS A BIG TUNNEL, MAW!

SURE IS, BOY! . . . WHAT WAS THAT NOISE?

GULP! S-S-S-SOUNDS L-L-LIKE A . . .

I'LL TELL YOU SOMETHIN' ELSE, BOY, IT LOOKS LIKE . . .

BAM!

POW!

A TRAIN! WE WERE ON THE MAIN LINE. THAT WEREN'T NO MINE SHAFT!

YOU'RE RIGHT AGAIN, MAW! HAA—AALP!

YONDER 70 MILES

THAT'LL BE FIFTY DOLLARS. WE DON'T LIKE PEOPLE WHO SNEAK RIDES.

THIS IS ALL YOUR FAULT, OSSIE. JUST WAIT UNTIL I GET MY HANDS ON YOU!

NOW, MAW, DON'T GO OFF THE RAILS!

When Olympic Bravery, a 276,000-ton oil tanker, went aground off the coast of Brittany, it was auctioned for scrap. There was one bid. A French dealer offered one franc—about 12p.

Football players and fans are on their best behaviour when referee David Atkins is in charge. A Class 1 whistler, appointed by Notts F.A., Brother David is a monk and travels to matches in his habit.

HOTSPUR HOTCH POTCH

OUR TAME ARTIST TAKES A NEW LOOK AT THE NEWS — AND THE NOT SO NEWS

Long-term prisoners in British jails are hooked on the matchstick model craze as a way of passing time. One man took several years to create a model of the Taj Mahal which required nearly 1,000,000 matches!

Oil pipeline workers in Alaska have to keep a close watch on their lunchtime sandwiches or goodies are scoffed by a cheeky thief—a large bear.

It took American artist John Banvard six years to complete the world's largest painting. The work which depicts the Mississippi River, is 5000 feet long by 12 feet deep.

Going for a dip in some parts of the United States can be a frustrating experience. Often the local fire brigades use the citizens' swimming pools as emergency water tanks.

VICTORIA CROSS CROSSING

IN 1868, after the railroad had been completed, the now thriving Western town of Victoria Cross was then Silver Gulch. A trestle bridge formed its approach crossing . . .

Hey, Limey! Git moving and help 'em unload.

Right, Mister Whitby. I'll get there right away!

Jim Cranton was English—a casual drifter . . .

That Cranton guy's half asleep half the time. He's just a deadbeat!

He ain't so bad! He's nervous. An' jumpy. But he's a good worker!

Move it, Limey! You heard the Boss!

Never seen such a frightened guy! Watch this! Should be good for a laugh!

Horses!

Ha! Ha! I told you this would be a laugh a minute!

It ain't much of a man who's scared o' horses.

Git back to sweeping streets, Limey! That's all you're good for!

No, it's all right! I— I'll give you a hand.

It—it wasn't always like this. Once I was good with horses. Please believe me.

Beat it! We've heard your tall tales before! How you was a hero in the cavalry an' all that!

They don't believe me. I suppose I can't blame them. A man's finished once he loses his nerve.

They ain't serving lemonade or lime juice today. You want a drink, go to the horse-trough.

I won't bother. I don't like trouble.

Jim turned away . . .

Don't you walk away from me, Limey. Hey, what's on that chain round your neck?

66

That's my business.

You sure talk big for a guy who's yellow! I ain't askin' twice. I'm gonna have a look!

Perhaps it was a lucky chance . . .

Oh, oh! Now we'll see real trouble!

Aargh!

I'll kill him! Give him a gun!

He can borrow my gun— seeing he won't need it for long!

Hold it right there, Red! I don't stand for murder!

You keep out of this, Rankine! Ain't none o' your business!

But—

Limey, run for my wagon! Red, don't try it!

You'll pay for this! You'll . . .

We got lucky. The sheriff's arrived.

Thanks! I owe you.

Forget it. Best I can do is take you to the next town or part way. That way, you may stay alive.

I wasn't always a coward—if that's what you're thinking!

None o' my business. But you sure ain't no hero!

The stagecoach should come this way soon. Get aboard and keep travelling an' stop telling them tall stories!

He's right—I'm no hero. Not now—not for a long time.

Jim waited but no stagecoach came...

I'll cross the river and try to get a job at the Bar Z ranch. I can't wait for ever. Never known the stage to be that late!

Later—

Smoke—a big fire! What's going on? Here comes a horse—and rider . . .

71

Before nightfall . . .

Hurrraaaaaay! They're retreating! They've had enough!

We owe that Limey plenty. Without him, we'd have been done for!

You'll never tell him. He's dead.

Red, the English guy didn't lie. We thought they were tall tales but they were true. He carried his proof. It was on the silver chain around his neck.

The Victoria Cross—awarded to Trooper J. Cranton for outstanding gallantry during the Crimean War. A hero and horseman.

And so . . .

I reckon we need more than this to show what we owe Jim Cranton. I'm sick at the way we misjudged him.

Don't worry, Red. There's one more honour we can give . . .

We'll call our township 'Victoria Cross Crossing'. He was one Englishman who should never be forgotten!

VICTORIA CROSS

IN MEMORY OF JIM CRANTON HORSEMAN AND HERO

THE END

73

HOW WAS I TO KNOW HE WAS A GENERAL?

You're in the wrong place, my man. The public bar is round the corner.

I fancy a spot of posh nosh so I'm in the right place, ain't I?

PRIVATE "PUNCHER" PAYNE, a top amateur heavyweight champion before the war, was a member of a special army unit known only as 'Company C'. After a long, hazardous mission behind the German lines, he had plenty of back pay in his pocket and he decided to treat himself to a meal in a big hotel. But . . .

I got the money to pay— so get out of my way!

Get out of here, at once! Common soliders are not allowed in The Carlton Room!

What's it to do with you, Fatso?

Fatso! Why I—

And what dinky little medals! Did you win them for war games with your toy soldiers, then?

So, next morning . . .

Quite a barney you had last night, Puncher, even by your standards.

But it wasn't my fault, sir! All I wanted was a bit of posh nosh.

Where you're going, Puncher, the nosh is far from posh. You see, the Army takes a poor view of privates punching Generals!

But how was I to know he was a General?

Well, you know now. I sentence you to one month's detention in a military prison. Dismiss him, Sergeant Major!

And so . . .

Maybe next time you meet General Livie, you'll salute him, instead of punching him, soldier!

But, a few days later, friends from 'Company C' approached the detention barracks . . .

MMMPH . . . AAARGH!

No offence, Sarge. We won't be too rough but we need to borrow one of our blokes back!

Come on, Puncher! Your little holiday's over! We've got work to do!

I don't care what it is, it'll be better than staying in here!

What's so important that you have to spring me out of here in such a hurry?

A General got himself shot down on the way to Sweden, and has been captured by the Germans in Norway.

That sounds like his bad luck. What's it got to do with me?

It's because you know him rather well.

Everything boyho. We've got to rescue him . . . and to make sure we get hold of the right man, you'll have to come along, see?

It's General Livie . . . the one you thumped in the Royal Hotel! Ha, ha, ha!

Twenty-four hours later, the three men from 'Company C' were parachuting down on to Norwegian soil. They were met by Norwegian Resistance men who took them to the luxury hotel where General Livie was held prisoner . . .

The German officers use that hotel as their headquarters. They have taken your General there.

It doesn't look too tight a prison. They're a bit too confident for their own good!

The patrolling sentries fell without a sound . . .

It don't seem all that long ago since we were doing this for you, boyho!

This General Livie bloke must be important for us to risk our necks to get him back!

You might say 'e's a bit snobby an' upper crust. But 'e's also one of the best military brains in Britain . . . He can win battles just by thinking about them!

77

Drop your guns and keep your mouth shut!

Now into the dining room! One word out o' you an you're dead!

No one move! We don't want no dead heroes!

Was is—?

That's Livie over there! Sitting down and eating with the Germans like he was one of them!

Time for you to escape, General!

I'm sorry, but I have been treated like a gentleman, and, in return, I have given my word not to escape!

This isn't a gentleman's war—an' I ain't no gentleman!

And this General's going to escape whether he wants to or not!

I told you—no heroes!

The Norwegian guide was ready with a horse drawn sledge . . .

That's the stuff, lads! Give 'em something to think about!

An aircraft had landed on the ice of a nearby lake . . .

Come on, General . . . we can't carry you all the way!

They were taken on to neutral Sweden . . . and the palatial British Embassy.

We'll be well looked after here, lads!

A splendid place. A life of luxury for us, look you!

Inside the entrance hall to the Embassy . . .

This way, please, General . . .

Thank you . . . and will you see that those men are taken to the servants' quarters . . .

No, boyho . . . you can't hit him again! Nobody gets a hat-trick of punches on a General.

Let me at that jumped-up—

After a few days of luxury living in Sweden, the General and the Company "C" men were flown back to Britain. They reported to their commanding-officer, Captain Darkbury . . .

I've got good news and bad news, Puncher! The bad news is that you'll have to complete the rest of your sentence. The good news is that they're not adding on any extra for the time you were out.

Generous of them—I don't think!

Stop pulling their legs, Darkbury! You know we can't keep men who win medals in detention!

The three of you have been awarded the Military Medal and the area Commanding General has decided that I should do the honours!

And so, a week later . . .

Well done, Private Payne! Thanks to you, I didn't have to break my word as an officer and a gentleman—even though you nearly broke my nose to do it!

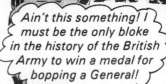

Ain't this something! I must be the only bloke in the history of the British Army to win a medal for bopping a General!

THE END

HURRICANE HUTCH

Move faster, Hutch or Canaria's hatchet man, El Tigre, will eat you on Saturday!

"Hurricane" Hutch Hutchinson and Ollie Peake of Midford City, had been selected to play for England against Canaria at Wembley for the Palata Cup. Hutch, the beefy, good-natured striker, became a soccer hurricane only when he was angry, it was always Ollie's job to get him going.

El Tigre's a soccer assassin. He's been suspended twice for brutal play.

I've heard all the horror stories about him, Ollie. Calm down! I'll make up my own mind about him when we meet.

But the England training session was being spied on.

El Tigre, don't upset the big number nine. That is Hutchinson.

The one nick-named Hurricane? He looks more like a bag of wind.

He's a gentle giant who becomes a hurricane if made angry. No defence can hold such a goal-scoring, net-breaking typhoon.

We take no chances, El Tigre. I have a plan to keep the hurricane gentle as a summer breeze!

After training—

A lovely day! I like jogging quietly back to our hotel.

You like everything. That's your trouble! Unless you really get going we'll lose to these blooming senors!

Look, Ollie, someone's rescuing a trapped kitten from that tree.

82

Here comes Hutchinson, just as we thought. We timed it nicely.

Can we help?

I don't believe it! That's El Tigre, the Canaria hatchet man!

He rescued the trapped kitten! So much for all those horror stories!

Gracias, amigo. So you too are an animal-lover?

Something fishy here! It's too good to be true!

I am proud to meet you, Big Hutch. It is sad that they call me 'El Tigre'. Me who would not hurt a kitten!

Don't worry about it. Actions speak louder than words!

Ollie, you should be ashamed of yourself spreading nasty rumours about that nice El Tigre.

They're all true! Don't be fooled by that act! He's rough, ruthless and nasty with it!

That rescue must have been a 'put up' job! I bet they expected us. It all happened too neatly.

You've a nasty, suspicious nature. I think El Tigre's one of nature's gentlemen.

The day of the match—

I've been looking forward to the duel between Hurricane Hutch and El Tigre.

It'll be some game! A battle of giants.

No tricks, Ollie. Don't try to turn me against El Tigre. He's a very nice chap!

You're barmy. He's an expert at sly fouls! It only ever shows if he loses his temper! Then he's murder!

Canaria opened strongly—

This lot will take some holding!

The referee missed El Tigre's first foul — a trip followed by a charge.

El Tigre made sure the ref was unsighted.

Ollie charged in—

OOOF! He's like a rock!

Ollie's up to his tricks. He's trying to make El Tigre look brutal.

A corner was awarded but Hutch's mind was elsewhere.

That was sporting of El Tigre to point out it was a corner. He's been badly misjudged.

Put a bit of effort into it, Hutch. You're playing like a great lemon.

You won't upset me, Ollie. You should try being a gentleman like El Tigre.

You dumb-dumb, El Tigre HAD to admit it was a corner! He knew the ref saw it.

You would say that! You really have your knife into El Tigre!

El Tigre's fouling was expert — and vicious . . .

Aaargh!

Look at that! El Tigre slammed Willie away with his elbow.

No, he didn't. El Tigre only jumped for the ball.

Goooaaaal!

Cunning brute! He made his dirty work pay off!

Nothing could get Hutch going and minutes later—

Three down! El Tigre distracted the goalie, but the ref didn't see him!

At half-time—

Rain! That's all we need. It'll make the pitch even wetter than you!

El Tigre's getting away with murder out there. He's used every clever, dirty trick in the book.

You see the worst of him because you expect it. Don't believe everything you read! Stop running him down.

The game restarted—

I can't stir up Hutch but perhaps I can get El Tigre going and make him show himself in his true colours.

Ollie tackled hard but—

OWWWW! My nose!

Don't put on your act for me, Ollie! I'm not fooled!

I'm not acting! He half killed me!

We've had it! El Tigre's too clever with the dirty work. Nothing will trigger Hutch off and we're done for without the hurricane!

MOUNTIE MULDOON

WATCH OUT FOR SALMON-POACHERS, THE SARGE SAID. AIN'T NONE AROUND THOUGH.

— HE'S AS DUMB AS THEY COME!

LIKEWISE, I GOTTA WATCH OUT FOR TWO DEER-POACHERS—BUT I DON'T RECKON THEY'RE AROUND RIGHT NOW!

I'LL CREEP ROUND THE BACK OF THE POLICE POST. MAYBE I CAN CATCH THE VILLAIN WHO'S BEEN ROBBING THE SERGEANT'S BEEHIVES!

E-E-E-Y-A-A-A-H!

HO-HO! HIM GOT-UM HEAD SAME-LIKE UM WAR-DRUM!

G-R-R-R-R! YOU WAIT TILL I GET MY HANDS ON YOU!

WAH! HE RUN SAME-LIKE -UM JACK-RABBIT!

YOU BETCHA!

93

THE BECKONING PEAK

IN 1941, Felice Benuzzi, an Italian, was put in a British prisoner-of-war camp in Kenya. He soon became fed-up of the same routine day after day. But there was nothing he could do to relieve the boredom – or was there?

MOUNT KENYA SEEMS TO BECKON TO ME. HOW WONDERFUL IT WOULD BE TO CLIMB IT—AND IT COULD BE DONE. IF I COULD BREAK OUT OF THIS PRISON CAMP AND—

Benuzzi put his plan to an experienced mountaineer, who scoffed.

YES, IT WOULD BE MOST ENJOYABLE TO GET OUT OF HERE AND UP INTO THE MOUNTAIN BUT IT COULDN'T BE DONE WITHOUT PORTERS AND ALL SORTS OF EQUIPMENT.

But Benuzzi persisted with his dream and others helped him, saving food and gathering supplies for the big day.

Equipment was made.

YOU MUST BE CRAZY. WHOEVER HEARD OF AN ICE AXE IN THE TROPICS?

At last all was ready for the attempt. On January 24, 1943, Benuzzi set out with a seaman called Enzo and a doctor called Giuan.

DON'T MAKE A SOUND! WE DON'T WANT THE GUARD TO HEAR US!

They struggled through thick jungle, hoping they wouldn't meet any savage animals. They had very little food and suffered terribly from the heat during the day and the cold at night. But, nine days after leaving the camp, they were on the lower slopes of the mountain. Enzo was too ill to continue, so Benuzzi and Giuan set off alone to climb the mountain.

THIS IS EVEN TOUGHER THAN I EXPECTED. PRISON LIFE IS NO PREPARATION FOR THIS SORT OF THING.

THESE AXES MAY BE HOME-MADE BUT THEY'RE AS GOOD AS ANYTHING MONEY CAN BUY! WE'RE MAKING GOOD TIME.

But later—

We must have been mad to leave our cosy, warm prison to die of frost-bite on the equator. We can't go on in this blizzard. We'll have to go back.

They returned to where Enzo had set up camp to wait for them.

It's not much, my friend, but at least it's hot and it is eaten in freedom!

When the blizzard stopped, they set out again. Many hours later—

Come, we are nearly there. Get the flag ready!

At last—

They said we were mad to try but we have made it.

I wonder if they can see our flag from the camp?

Their moment of triumph over, they wearily made their way down the mountain—a task even more dangerous than the ascent and made even more difficult by their weakened condition.

Once off the mountain, they started trekking through difficult and sometimes dangerous country as they headed back towards captivity.

Watch out for buffalo. Some say he's the most dangerous animal in the jungle.

Later—

Quiet. We are nearly back at the camp. It is a matter of honour that we get in without being discovered.

Soon—

Back home at last.

The commander will get a shock in the morning.

Next day, in the Commanding Officer's office—

This is a real rum do. Fancy people breaking out of prison camp just to climb a mountain.

The prison camp Commander was so amazed that he sentenced the prisoners to only a few days in the cells. Untrained and ill-equipped, the Italian prisoners-of-war had gone chasing a dream and had climbed one of the world's great mountains to complete a feat unique in military and mountaineering history!

See, the mountain beckons again. It is because of it I am in this cell, but the few days of freedom on the mountain were worth years of captivity.

IT'S A FUNNY OLD WORLD

Two lions once escaped from a railway wagon in a Budapest station. One attacked Istvan Kristof and pinned him to the ground. Lion tamer, Sandor Komlos, bit the lion's nose and it released the terrified man.

Dutch seagulls once came under attack from Treytel, goalkeeper of the crack football team, Feyenoord, who brought one down with a goal kick.

Many daring escapes were attempted during the First World War. One quick-witted Frenchman escaped the Germans by hiding in a piano case.

A man in Oklahoma was sentenced to 39 days in prison but ate so much the sheriff let him out before his sentence was completed.

American convict, Walter Brown, pretended to be sweeping a corridor. Straight over the courtyard and past the guards he went — and made a clean getaway.

A baby elephant in a British zoo wouldn't keep quiet at night and keepers couldn't get to sleep. Then a cure was discovered. A night light was put in the elephant's cage and there was peace at last. Jumbo was scared in the dark!

There are very unusual schools in Montreal, Canada. The pupils are dogs which are taught to understand commands in both English and French.

The wettest football match played every year is at Bourton-on-the-Water in the Cotswolds. Goals are set up between two bridges on the River Windrush. The pitch — is the river itself!

Australian escapologist, Murray Walters, is a cool one. He once wriggled out of a strait jacket whilst lying in a lion's cage in a circus.

KING COBRA

ACE, free-lance Newsman, Bill King, was in the outback of Australia to write up a rash of mysterious killings . . .

Red Gap coming up, sports. It s only claim to fame is that it is riddled with a cave system said to hide a lode of pure gold. They call it Logan's Lost Reef!

Gold and killings always go together—but I'm going to get to the bottom of this lot!

I've just booked in at the Gap Hotel, Mister Kline.

Better not run up too big a bill, King. And, remember, it's the supernatural aspect that interests the New York Monitor!

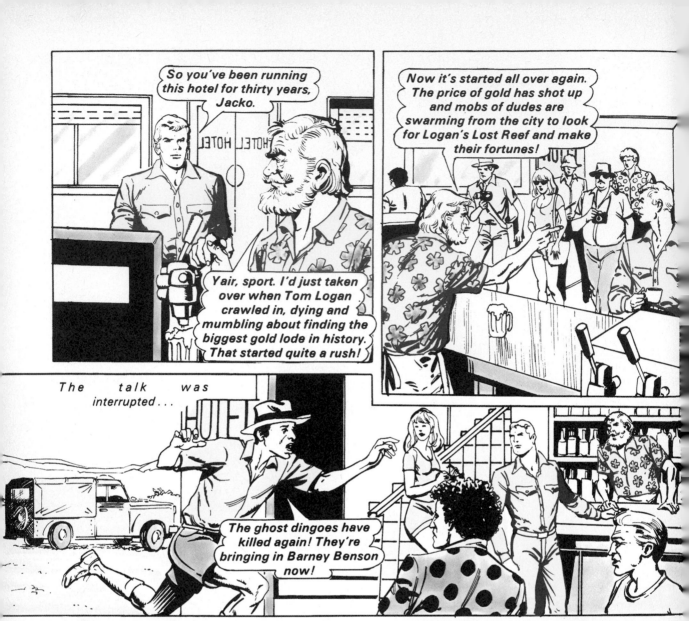

So you've been running this hotel for thirty years, Jacko.

Yair, sport. I'd just taken over when Tom Logan crawled in, dying and mumbling about finding the biggest gold lode in history. That started quite a rush!

Now it's started all over again. The price of gold has shot up and mobs of dudes are swarming from the city to look for Logan's Lost Reef and make their fortunes!

The talk was interrupted . . .

The ghost dingoes have killed again! They're bringing in Barney Benson now!

Me and Barney was chipping samples in the blue vault when they come at us—a pack of dingoes, all shining white and eyes like fire . . .

POLICE POST

I got away, but Barney was pulled down . . .

"Trooper Pringle, when are the police going to do something about them ghost dingoes? We need protection!"

The hotel refilled . . .

"Right now, chum. I'm putting the caves out of bounds till this matter's been investigated."

"Don't blame the trooper, blokes. There ain't much just one officer can do when he's up against the Mamu. That's what the blackfellows call the ghost dingoes that guard the Great Mindi, the spirit snake of the underworld."

"That's the legend, boys. You won't get an Abo go anywhere near them caves."

"Anybody would think Jacko was trying to scare customers away from the caves!"

In the night, Bill slipped out for a stroll . . .

OUT OF BOUNDS POLICE NOTICE

"Here's where I change into my gear. I'll need my infra-red peepers."

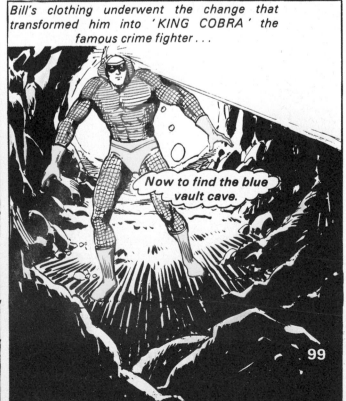

Bill's clothing underwent the change that transformed him into 'KING COBRA' the famous crime fighter . . .

"Now to find the blue vault cave."

So this is where the ghost dingoes hang out when they're not killing people! They seem harmless enough right now!

What's this? Looks like one of those control units for model aircraft.

Those collars on the animals must carry receivers for a signal rigged to cause pain!

The ghost pack suddenly erupted ferociously . . .

I switched it on and look at those dingoes now!

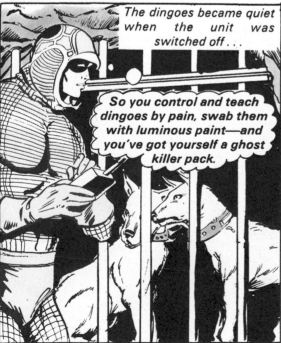

The dingoes became quiet when the unit was switched off . . .

So you control and teach dingoes by pain, swab them with luminous paint—and you've got yourself a ghost killer pack.

I got out of there just in time. Somebody is coming!

It's Jacko, the genial host of the Gap Hotel!

Jacko met King Cobra...

I suppose you are here to visit your pets.

The Mindi snake! Thunderation, that Abo legend's true after all!

Keep away—aargh!

A torch lit the night...

Hey, you in the funny rig! What's going on here?

It's not often you have a policeman turn up just when he's needed. I suggest you look in that cave, Trooper Pringle.

I'll look, but you stay right where you are, Mister Mindi—or whoever you are!

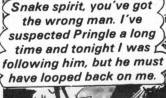

Snake spirit, you've got the wrong man. I've suspected Pringle a long time and tonight I was following him, but he must have looped back on me.

Trooper Pringle's crazy! The dreamtime's got him.

The SLOWEST GUN in the WEST

IN the 1870's, the Royal Artillery presented to the U.S. Army one of the Iron Duke's famous cannon. Sergeant-Major Fry and Gunner Mullins were detailed to deliver the old gun to Fort Grabb, in the Arizona territory . . .

Permission to speak, sir! Looks like a storm coming.

Bad weather don't generally travel on four hoofs, Gunner.

Stand firm, Gunner. All animals fear the steady stare of the human eye.

If you say so, sir.

Though American animals may be different.

Yessir. Just as you say, sir! SHHHH!

Let's get outa this bushwhack.

Pour it into them lawhawks, boys. Show 'em they'll only get their feathers scorched taking on Lobo Slim.

Fry had established an observation post . . .

'Orrible bungled business. I'd better see how the Gunner's getting on with that little fatigue I gave him.

Gunner, make sure you trim them trees nice and tidy when you've dropped them.

Yessir.

The defeated posse shambled back . . .

We'll pitch camp in that cottonwood grove.

Hey, Sheriff, look what's coming.

You greenhorns had better turn off or you'll be heading up to Buzzard's Roost.

Precisely, sir. We have to recover two horses, property of Her Majesty's forces.

Mullins did some climbing...

Get a move on, Gunner.

Yessir.

...then some hauling...

...and more hauling...

Take note how my notion of a sheer-legs eases your task, Gunner.

Yessir. Very good of you, sir.

Next the block-trail and then we'll haul up the wheels.

Sundown ended a busy day...

Gunner, you may assemble gun and limber while I scout the locality.

Very good, sir.

Two bandits left on guard at the head of the defile.

The high meadowland where stolen stock is pastured. Good grass . . . well watered . . . and that must be the roost of the buzzards . . .

Dusk settled . . .

The police party is settled for the night. Most sensible of them not to risk blundering about in an assault by darkness. Night manoeuvres is best left to the military.

Dawn brought a noisy awakening to Buzzard's Roost . . .

I tell you that was artillery, Lobo. I heard enough in the war.

WHACK!

BOOM

Nah! A bit o' thunder more like!

Fry had fired a ranging round . . .

Plus five degrees and we are on target, Gunner. How is that shot cooking?

Nice and hot, sir!

Having only roundshot or canister calls for improvising, Gunner. Now, it so happens that hotted shot is very effective against masts, rigging, wooden hulls and such like timber structures!

The 9-pounder came on-target . . .

BOOOM!

There it goes again—an' it is artillery!

The piece is up on that rimrock. Let's go get it.

We're with yuh, Lobo.

Fry was observing . . .

The hostiles are commencing a flanking movement. Gunner, make a switch of thirty degrees to the right.

We shall load with canister shot.

The rustlers reached the guard post . . .

Over that way, boys.

BOooOM!

Thar it is!

A storm of leaden balls broke about the attackers . . .

YEEEOW

Ahhhh!

WHAM!

THANG!

YEOWH!

PING!

THE GLOSTER GLADIATOR

IN 1940, British forces in Norway depended on Gladiators of 263 Squadron, R.A.F. for air support. One day, Flying Officer Jacobsen on solo patrol, saw a mixed force of German bombers coming in over the Swedish border.

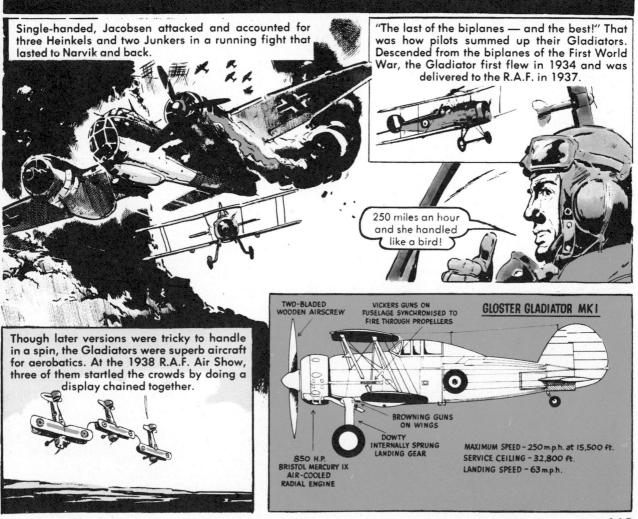

Single-handed, Jacobsen attacked and accounted for three Heinkels and two Junkers in a running fight that lasted to Narvik and back.

"The last of the biplanes — and the best!" That was how pilots summed up their Gladiators. Descended from the biplanes of the First World War, the Gladiator first flew in 1934 and was delivered to the R.A.F. in 1937.

250 miles an hour and she handled like a bird!

Though later versions were tricky to handle in a spin, the Gladiators were superb aircraft for aerobatics. At the 1938 R.A.F. Air Show, three of them startled the crowds by doing a display chained together.

GLOSTER GLADIATOR MK I

TWO-BLADED WOODEN AIRSCREW

VICKERS GUNS ON FUSELAGE SYNCHRONISED TO FIRE THROUGH PROPELLERS

BROWNING GUNS ON WINGS

DOWTY INTERNALLY SPRUNG LANDING GEAR

850 H.P. BRISTOL MERCURY IX AIR-COOLED RADIAL ENGINE

MAXIMUM SPEED – 250 m.p.h. at 15,500 ft.
SERVICE CEILING – 32,800 ft.
LANDING SPEED – 63 m.p.h.

When war broke out in 1939, the Gladiators were being replaced by Hurricanes and Spitfires, but 250 of the biplanes went into action against the Germans, destroying an average of more than one enemy aircraft each, during the first six months of battle.

A Gladiator of 603 (City of Edinburgh) Squadron scored one of the first victories of the war, downing an intruder into the River Forth.

The Gladiators fought their first major campaign in Norway. A squadron flew 180 miles from an aircraft carrier through a blinding snowstorm—

What a blizzard! We can't keep formation in this stuff! Let's hope we get to base soon!

Base for the Gladiators of 263 Squadron was a frozen lake. In two days, the gallant biplanes destroyed 30 enemy bombers.

Squadron Leader J. W. Donaldson, who led the Gladiators, won the D.S.O. and three D.F.C.'s and one Military Medal went to 263 Squadron pilots.

One of the most famous stories of the Gladiators is the defence of Malta, also in 1940. When the Italian Air Force was trying to bomb the island into surrender, only a handful of Sea Gladiators flew in its defence.

Here they come again! Let's go and meet them!

A pity the old Glads are too slow to catch the bombers — but we'll give 'em a fright.

Three Gladiators, known as "Faith", "Hope" and "Charity", held off the Italian threat. Later, when the Luftwaffe started using Stukas to pound Malta . . .

Stukas are at their weakest when they're pulling out of their dives! That's when this beauty with two extra guns will hit them!

She'll taste Stuka blood all right!

In memory of the part Gladiators played in the defence of Malta, one battered biplane, labelled "Faith", was set up in the Palace of the Grand Masters.

But the Gladiators story does not end at Malta. The Italian Air Force also struck treacherously at Greece. On the 28th February, 1941, 28 Gladiators and Hurricanes took part in one of the R.A.F.'s greatest fights, destroying 27 out of a total of 50 Italian fighters and bombers in 90 minutes of concentrated action.

In this action all the Gladiators suffered was one forced landing.

I'm lucky to get out of that. Now for a long walk back to base! I want to be back in action by tomorrow.

One ace who flew Gladiators was Flight Lieutenant "Pat" Pattle, who before he was posted missing, was one of the R.A.F.'s top scorers, with over 30 victories, most of them gained in six months' Gladiators flying.

A South African, Pattle was awarded the Distinguished Flying Cross — twice.

The Gladiators even went into action with swastikas painted on them when the Finns used them against the Russians in 1940.

The Gladiator finished its career in the Middle East and the days of wires, struts and fixed undercarriages were over. After two years of action against faster and more heavily armed adversaries the biplanes had earned a special place in flying history.

OUR FINNY FRIENDS
The Dolphins

PELORUS JACK was the name given to a dolphin which guided ships through a safe channel in the treacherous straits between d'Urville Island and Nelson Province in New Zealand.

Dolphins seem to regard human beings as friends. One drowning Japanese fisherman was rescued by a school of dolphins which pulled and pushed him into shallower water.

Porpoises are a smaller version of dolphins but can swim at over 30 miles per hour. A school of them, cornered by scientists in a narrow Florida inlet, leapt high into the air over the boat blocking their escape route.

Opo, a wild dolphin, freqently entered Oponomi Bay, New Zealand, to play with the swimmers, allowing children to ride on its back.

Dolphins amaze crowds at dolphinariums all over the world and have even been trained to jump through rings of fire.

But dolphins aren't used solely to amuse the public. They are highly intelligent creatures and have been taught to carry tools to divers on the sea-bed.

American scientists taught a dolphin to understand the difference between hundreds of symbols on a blackboard. Later, it scored 84 per cent in an exam by tapping out the answers on the board with its snout. Dolphins have a language of their own and scientists are trying to decipher it. Perhaps, some day, man will be able to hold conversations with his finny friends.

... The Insect Master! Warped, brilliant and driven by some private hate.

What's going on? What's that — no-o-o!

It's a hold-up! The Insect Master's after the mail train's 'high-value' coaches. He always hits Government Agencies!

Nothing can stop it! Look out!

Run for your life!

It's taken the high-value bags — and there's nothing we can do about it!

The metal brute has to be guided in some way. Maybe I can 'blind' it!

I'll have to use the homing device. Mission cancelled! X-Bow, you'll pay.

It's worked! The Beetle is burrowing off — empty-handed!

So long, guys! My job's over!

If I play my cards right, I'll make the Insect Master unhappier still. I'll try to force him into the open.

Two nights later . . .

The best way to find out what he could be after next is to ask other criminals — and I might as well choose the top hoodlum!

Correlli was an Underworld Boss . . .

Sorry, I didn't fancy the front door!

Holy crow—!

Don't move! You mightn't live to regret it!

Corelli, if you wanted to rip off the U.S. Government in a hurry, what heist would you pull? Something big and spectacular . . .

The South American gold shipment on Wednesday. Ingots — escorted. The army will be there. It would be suicide to try it!

Thanks! That's all I wanted to know!

Tranquilliser gas hissed out . . .

Sleep well. I'll leave by the door this time!

Aargh!

On Wednesday . . .

The gold shipment's arrived. I hope my journey has been necessary!

There are enough troops to repel an invasion. I'm having doubts . . .

Suddenly . . .

Look out! What in—

Giant hornets! It ain't possible!

Paralysing gas was released . . .

Remote-controlled! More of the Insect Master's robots!

Aargh!

My only chance is to jam the radio control signal!

If they detect me before I hit them, I'm done for!

Far away . . .

Kill him! Kill him! He's jamming the signals . . .

The deadly hornets went out of control . . .

Lucky for me, I got in first!

oops recovered . . .

Time to leave. This should really upset the Insect Master!

This is the last time you'll interfere, X-Bow. I'm looking for you. "I want you in my web," said the spider to the fly!

Corelli contacted X-Bow days later . . .

I'm ready! You've got to be prepared when you know you're riding into a trap!

I've heard a buzz — your friend could hit the Government meat-packing plant at pier thirteen. Tomorrow night . . .

Here comes the bait for the Insect Master's trap! Never trust an enemy!

Without warning . . .

Blazing light! Ah, it's blinding me!

Before he could brake . . .

A giant web!

. . . X-Bow was held fast!

n explosive bolt flew . . .

. . . right down its throat!

No, you don't! I want you, friend.

He jumped. I've missed . . .

He hasn't come up. Only bubbles . . . perhaps it's for the best!

Later . . . Tell the Government I don't think they'll be bothered further. I found his control complex — oh, and what spare cash there was lying about, I kept!

I'll forget that last part . . .

Next week-end . . .

Mister, how can you afford to train us for free?

A money-spider brought me luck!

The End

The Supermarine Spitfire was the smallest fighter that could be designed to carry eight machine guns, a retractable undercarriage and an enclosed cockpit around a Rolls Royce PV-12 engine.

Nineteen R.A.F. squadrons were equipped with Spitfire 1's at the outbreak of the Battle of Britain. They were faster and more manoeuvrable than their Messerschmitt Bf 109E opponents but were out-gunned, out-climbed and out-dived by the German machines.